SWATI SENGUPTA is an author and journalist. Her books include *Out of War* (Speaking Tiger Books 2016), *Guns on My Red Earth* (Rupa, 2013), *Half the Field Is Mine* (Scholastic, 2014), *The Talking Bird* (Tulika Books, 2014) and *A Tea Garden Party* (Pratham Books, 2021). She translated *Murder In The City* (Speaking Tiger Books, 2018) from Bengali to English. Swati runs a workshop series on gender for young adults. She studied English at Jadavpur University and lives in Kolkata.

Also in the series by Swati Sengupta:

Jhalkari Bai: The Braveheart Warrior
Milkha Singh: The Runner Who Could Fly
Savitribai Phule: The Fearless Reformer

The Incredible Life of
Birsa Munda
The Great Revolutionary Leader

Swati Sengupta

Illustrations by Devashish Verma

An Imprint of Speaking Tiger Books

TALKING CUB

Published by Speaking Tiger Books LLP
125A, Ground Floor, Shahpur Jat,
Near Asiad Village, New Delhi 110 049

First published in paperback in Talking Cub
by Speaking Tiger Books in 2023

Text copyright © Swati Sengupta 2023

Illustration copyright © Speaking Tiger Books 2023

ISBN: 978-93-5447-440-8

eISBN: 978-93-5447-472-9

10 9 8 7 6 5 4 3 2 1

Typeset in Georgia by Jojy Philip
Printed at Shree Maitrey Printech Pvt. Ltd., Noida

No part of this publication may be reproduced, transmitted, or stored in a retrieval system, in any form or by any means, electronic, mechanical, photocopying, recording or otherwise, without the prior permission of the publisher.

This book is sold subject to the condition that it shall not, by way of trade or otherwise, be lent, resold, hired out, or otherwise circulated, without the publisher's prior consent, in any form of binding or cover other than that in which it is published.

For Kajori

Chapter One

As dusk descended in the forest, the birds returned home to the tall sal trees. But they weren't chirping. Instead, they seemed to be listening to the sweet music of the tuila playing at a distance. When Birsa, the Munda boy, played his one-stringed tuila, the birds and animals of the forest stayed still and listened, enchanted. His music could even move mountains, people said!

Not a leaf stirred as Birsa played the tuila, which was made out of pumpkin shell, bamboo, dry wood and cotton yarn. Birsa could also play the flute. He was an unusual boy. Birds, animals, trees and humans would be mesmerized when he

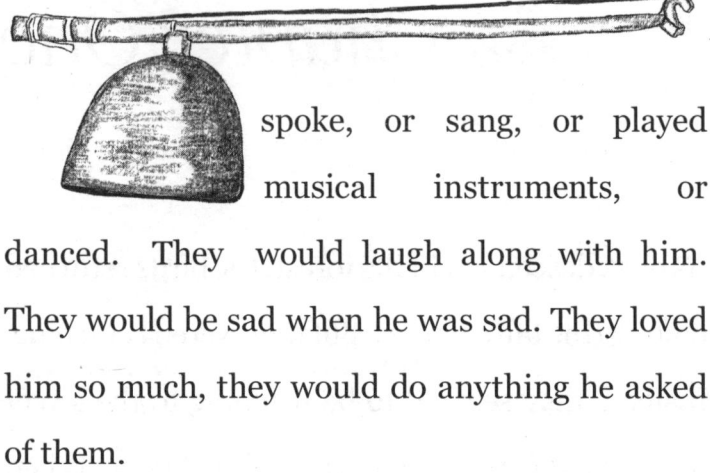

spoke, or sang, or played musical instruments, or danced. They would laugh along with him. They would be sad when he was sad. They loved him so much, they would do anything he asked of them.

Years later, when Birsa was a youth, his people listened to his words and joined him in raising their voices against oppression and exploitation. He led them in a people's movement, demanding their rights. It was a great ulgulan (a movement) that would be remembered forever.

Years before Birsa was born, a young man named Sugana, and his wife Karmi Munda, roamed these forests. They had few belongings and built huts with bamboo strips and mud plasters wherever they hoped to find some work. Sugana was born in Ulihatu, which is now in the state of Jharkhand. Thickly forested Ulihatu has hills, hillocks and beautiful streams that flow tirelessly, making beautiful music with their gurgling waters. There are biting cold winter nights and burning summer days here.

Sugana and Karmi moved from one village to the next in search of work as ryots or sajhadars. They worked as hired labourers who tilled the land for the landowners.

During the years that they moved from one village to another in search of work, they had three sons—Komta, Kanu, Birsa—and two daughters—Daskir and Champa. They worked hard all day in the forests and farms for their livelihood.

Their son Birsa, the hero of our story, was born in the early 1870s. The exact date of his birth is not clear, nor is the exact place of his birth. Was it 18 July 1872? Or was it 15 November 1875? Some say that he was born on a Thursday and was named after the day of his birth, according to the Munda custom. Was he born in Ulihatu or was it Bamba? There are differences of opinion on this too. The more popular view is that he was born in Ulihatu on 15 November 1875.

> History often contains these contradictions. Some facts are recorded in government reports and personal notes and these are generally thought of as more 'authentic' or real. Sometimes events or incidents are available only in songs and stories passed on from one person to another over years and generations. This is known as oral history. There is no reason to believe that oral history is any less real or important than recorded facts.

The story of Birsa Munda is a combination of written records and oral history. The scant records are backed by the vibrant songs of the Mundas and stories about him that have now become folklore—often a mix of actual events and myths.

When Birsa was born, the family moved to Chalkad, Sugana's mother's village. Birsa grew up here. Chalkad is in the Khunti district and the nearest big town is Ranchi. Part of the South Chhotanagpur division, Khunti is one of the twenty-four districts of Jharkhand state.

Jharkhand itself is quite young. It was formed out of Bihar on 15 November 2000. The date is significant as it was chosen for being Birsa Munda's birth anniversary.

Birsa's birth ceremony was performed in Chalkad. 'Look at the smiling face! Look at those sparkling eyes! This boy will do something great,' many remarked as they came to bless the little baby.

The Mundas are an ethnic group in India, who speak the Mundari language. They are one of India's largest scheduled tribes. The Mundas believe in a supreme being they call Sing Bonga. He is revered and invoked during calamities. Two lesser classes of deities (bongas) are the village gods and the household gods. The village priest, pahan, presides over the worship of these gods at the sacred grove in the village. Several other gods and spirits are worshipped, too. Animals are sacrificed to the gods. Over the years, some Mundas have adopted Hinduism and Christianity.

Birsa's uncle, his father's elder brother, had converted to Christianity before Birsa was born. After Birsa's birth, Sugana and Sugana's younger brother became Christians as well. Sugana then became a catechist of the German mission—a teacher who spreads the messages and teachings of Christianity. Locally, catechists were known as pracharaks. Birsa was also converted to Christianity through baptism. His father's name, after his conversion, became Masih Das, and Birsa became Daud Munda or Daud Birsa.

During this time, in this region, the missionaries often acted as a bridge between the British officers and the Adivasis. If the Adivasi people disagreed with the government, they would write to the British officers, and the missionaries would help them in this.

As a child, Birsa experienced extreme poverty. Most of the time, there was nothing to eat. They would eat ghato, a gruel or thick soup made out of boiled china grass but the stomach always ached with hunger.

How he dreamed of eating a plateful of rice! The beautiful white or slightly brown grains, when boiled with water, filled the air with such a sweet smell. The steam from utensils of boiling rice made him giddy with excitement. He imagined filling his fist with the soft, hot grains and squeezing them between his fingers, forming little balls that he would toss into his mouth. Aah! The hungry tummy would be soothed and sleep would overpower him immediately. How wonderful it must be to eat lots of rice and doze off to sleep. But eating rice was a luxury.

Seeing their condition, Birsa's mother's sister asked Sugana if she could take him with her.

Sugana could not say no. Actually, it would help if he didn't have another person to feed.

At his aunt's home, a young Birsa loved exploring the forests and fields. Dressed in a loincloth and covering his head with another tiny piece of cloth, he would set out in the morning to graze goats and sheep. Sometimes, he would take the

cattle of his aunt's family, and sometimes from rich people who paid the family for the work Birsa did. He would take them out through the forest, his flute tied to the waist. He would also carry with him the tuila.

The flute and tuila by his side, Birsa would lay on the grass while the animals happily had their fill of the juicy fresh grass. Birsa also loved to play. Often, he would roll on the dust and sand, laughing wildly. Sometimes, people said, the Munda boy spoke of strange things that they could not understand.

One day, something terrible happened. As the goats were grazing, he noticed that one of them had gone missing. Some wild animal may have quietly snatched it away. Now there would be trouble. Birsa's fears came true. He was beaten black and blue by his aunt's husband.

His little body hurt. What he felt inside was even worse. The world had hunger, poverty and there was no love. Crying would not help. He would have to *act*. Birsa decided to run away. He would go back to his parents. There was no need for food. He would die of hunger, but he would not let them beat him anymore.

When Birsa returned to his parents, Sugana Munda was both happy and sad to see his son. He had missed his dear Birsa. But how could he bring up this child? How could he feed him? Sugana soon decided to send Birsa to Ayubhatu, which was Birsa's mother's village and where his maternal uncle lived.

Birsa hoped there would be food and no

beatings there. He didn't want much, anyway. Hoping for a better life, Birsa set off for Ayubhatu, which was close by.

Near Ayubhatu, there was a school, at a place called Salga. Here there were books, and proper rooms where students sat and listened to teachers who taught many things. There were other boys his age, there was food and here was a great opportunity to escape the sorrows of the world. Birsa had an imaginative mind. He was a dreamer. Often, he would get lost in imaginary lands and fought imaginary battles.

The school at Salga was run by Jaipal Nag. He was highly respected and took good care of the schoolchildren, told them stories, and made them aware of the world around. It was from Nag that Birsa learned who the British were, how big the world outside their villages was, and so much more! Nag had a huge influence on the little Birsa Munda.

Birsa understood that his own life, and that of many others around him, was filled with miserable poverty and uncertainties. The lessons in school made him understand the rights of the Adivasis, what the British were doing, and the power of the landlords and zamindars.

Adivasis had always been an integral part of the forests. But the British sahibs and some rich landlords were encroaching into their land. The Adivasis, now, were without land or livelihood, and were always hungry. Like Birsa's parents, they were compelled to go from one place to another to earn a living. The landlords were rich and had the support of British rulers. Both had come from outside and taken over their land.

This upset Birsa very much. He wondered what he could do to change it.

Birsa was in Ayubhatu for two years. After he studied lower primary at the Salga school and a German mission at Burju, it was time to take up higher or upper primary studies. Students in the hilly areas of southern Khunti and Tamar would go to Chaibasa, a distance of approximately 100 kilometres, for this. Birsa was sent to a German Lutheran Mission school in Chaibasa for high school where he stayed in a hostel.

There, he studied Western history, modern science and English language, among other subjects. These were all about new ideas, histories of far-off lands, modern scientific developments, social revolutions and literature. The local children learned about the need to educate themselves and to explore new lands and ideas through their books. But there is another aspect to education. When we learn, we also learn to question.

Birsa Munda, who was exceptionally sharp and intelligent, felt that perhaps those imparting education among the poor Adivasi people were exploiting them too. Perhaps the British should not rule over them. Why did their homes never have enough food? Why were they burdened with taxes? Why were some people rich while the Adivasis always remained impoverished?

These questions bothered Birsa no end. School

lessons helped him understand the plight of his people, and the exploitation and oppression by British rulers.

What had been happening to the Mundas and other Adivasis to make him think this way?

Chapter Two

The Adivasis lived in the forests and depended on it for food. For this, they cleared parts of the forests and turned them into agricultural land. Among them were the Mundas, who are said to have settled in the Chhotanagpur region after coming down from the north-west and were earlier a wandering group of people. The word 'Munda' is said to have come from a Sanskrit word meaning 'headman', and it was an honorific title that became the name of the community. The land, forest and everything in it belonged to them collectively. The idea of 'personal property' was not important for the Mundas.

Soon, these lands produced wonderful crops and came to be known as 'fertile' land.

But as the Mundas developed connections with the outside world, moneylenders used various tricks to usurp their land. Their lack of literacy was a disadvantage, and they held no written documents of their lands. Thus they got into debts, their land was taken away and many became bonded labourers. The land that once belonged to them was where they started working for others, against little or no money.

The khuntkatti system was the ancient land settlement system in this area. In this system, land was owned collectively based on lineage. But this system was gradually disrupted by the coming of outsiders. It created new rifts as the land ownership shifted, and with the coming of the British Raj, a new tax collection system led to further exploitation.

The British East India Company had gained control over large areas of the subcontinent by the late 1700s. They introduced the Permanent Settlement first in Bengal and Bihar and subsequently all over northern India. In this system, Indian landowners, or zamindars, collected taxes for the East India Company. This eventually led to the Adivasis losing their traditional rights over the land on which they depended for their livelihood. The rents and taxes the Adivasi peasants had to pay were very high and sometimes they were even forced to work in others' land as they got into debt.

Many Adivasis protested this exploitation, and thus, several protests or uprisings took place in Bengal (now West Bengal and Bangladesh), Jharkhand and Orissa (now Odisha).

> One of the first Adivasi protests against the British was by Tilka Manjhi, an Adivasi leader who fought the British in 1784.
>
> Later, the Kol insurrection occurred between 1830 and 1833 in Chhotanagpur, and the Bhumij revolt of Manbhum in 1832-33. There was the Santhal rebellion of 1855, the Munda revolt of Ranchi in 1889, and the Sardar uprising in Ranchi in 1894-95.
>
> Among these, the Santhal uprising under the leadership of Sidho Murmu and Kanhu Murmu, in 1855-56, was perhaps the biggest. The Santhals with their bows and arrows and other primitive weapons waged war against the British imperialists.

When Birsa was a child, the Sardar movement was on. The Sardars believed that 'the Adivasis were the first people to clear the lands of Chhotanagpur and thus they had the truest rights to free access to the Chhotanagpur land'. Theirs was a peaceful protest. It was in the form of petitions or appeals before the British government officials, where they spoke of restoring land to the Adivasis. They made strong and consistent appeals to British officers, including the Viceroy of India and the secretary of state for India in London. This took place between 1858 and 1895.

In this, the Sardars were helped by the Christian missionaries. However, the Sardars soon felt that these petitions to the British government were not helping them much. So they began to file court suits against the missionaries and the Christian Adivasis who appeared in court on behalf of the British.

The missionaries and their preachers often told the Adivasis that they might get all their land back if they continued to pray. But the reality was different. Nothing changed.

Birsa was well aware of land rights and taxes. He had noticed that the authorities of the missionary school were opposed to the idea of the Mundas demanding their land rights. During one of the classes, Dr Notrott spoke against the Munda struggle. All the students were listening silently, but Birsa grew more and more angry. He tried to quell his anger but after a while he could not take it any more and stood up to protest. 'What you are saying is wrong!' Birsa said. There! He had said it! It felt good. A huge weight seemed to have got lifted. He felt light after this act of defiance.

He knew that this would have consequences and that he would be expelled from school. He didn't want to go on studying in the school either. He felt that he could no longer continue to be selfish and care only about his own future when his people were in such distress.

Birsa left the mission school knowing that it would mean an uncertain life yet again. No more meals at the school hostel, no more education. It meant plunging into darkness. While leaving the Chaibasa school, his angry outburst was: *'saheb, saheb ek topi hai'* (all the foreigners—British and the missionaries—wear the same cap).

Birsa was right. Walking away from the missionary school proved a major turning point.

It was the beginning of who he became later in life. It shaped his ideas and thoughts. From now on, he saw himself as one of those being exploited, like his entire community—and that it was the government and the missionaries exploiting them.

Birsa had lived in Chaibasa from 1886 to 1890. The agitation of the Sardars was going on not far from his school there. This also deeply influenced him, and perhaps prompted his decision to leave school.

It's not easy for a young boy to leave high school, knowing he would have to start earning a living now. It is even more tough to leave school in protest. But the first spark had shown itself. Birsa was capable of taking tough decisions.

After he left Chaibasa in 1890, Birsa and his family gave up their membership of the German mission.

Birsa initially returned to his family. But once back there, he came face to face with another harsh reality. Superstition was common among the villagers, as was drinking and the killing of animals for religious sacrifice. Birsa's missionary school education had taught him the value of science and the need to get rid of superstitions. He understood that it would be tough to flush out age-old practices and he had to wait for the right moment. But now he knew—a sweeping change was needed.

Birsa set off for Bandgaon, less than 100 kilometres from Chaibasa, looking for work. Here, apart from working as an agricultural labourer, he also came across something that further shaped his ideas. It was another religion: Vaishnavism.

> Vaishnavism is a religious belief based on the worship of Lord Vishnu (or one of his various incarnations). There are various Vaishnav groups, and one of the most influential in the Chhotanagpur region was the one started by Chaitanya Mahaprabhu, a 15th-century saint. He spoke—through song and music—of a divine and pure love, devotion, equality and against divisions of caste.

Birsa stayed with Anand Panre, who worked as a manager of a landlord in Bandgaon. During the day, Birsa worked in the fields, and in the evenings, he studied and had a number of discussions with Panre, who had vast knowledge of Vaishnavism. Soon, Birsa was enthralled by the songs and taken in by the idea of devotion. He was so engrossed in the ideas that he even started dreaming about them.

At Bandgaon, Birsa saw even more closely the stark contrast in the lifestyle of people. While the landlords lived in luxury, the poor peasants had almost nothing to eat!

During the three years he lived in Bandgaon, Birsa also got more directly involved in an agitation to protest restrictions on the Mundas' traditional rights over forest land. What Birsa understood was this: the land policies of the British were destroying their traditional land system, and the zamindars and moneylenders were taking over their land, while the missionaries were criticizing them for protesting against this.

After three years, enriched as well as ravaged by his experiences, Birsa eventually returned to Chalkad. Now he was soon to emerge as a prophet and hero and lead the Adivasis' fight. He turned the mild protests of the Sardars into a forceful and powerful movement against the British imperialists, one of the first such movements that would, much later, lead to India's Independence in 1947.

How did something as momentous as this take place?

Chapter Three

The Munda leaders had decided to not pay taxes to the landlords. What they did not realize was that the British government would join hands with the landlords. The courts turned down the Adivasis' plea and the Sardar movement suffered a setback.

Around 1894-95, the Sardars' movement was almost dying down due to pressure from the British. A large number of Mundas were arrested and charged with stirring people against the government. Around this time, Birsa organized the peasants of six neighbouring villages and submitted a memorandum in Chaibasa town. But the government paid no heed. It was clearer than ever that the enemy was not just the landlords, but the British too. And any movement protesting their plights should not leave out the British.

Along with this, Birsa felt that the Mundas needed something good to happen to them from *within.* Something they could be hopeful about. What else could bring this about but religion—the idea of Jesus Christ, Lord Vishnu, the ecstasy of songs, the hopefulness and cheer of carols. It should not be something that depressed the poor Mundas further. Yes, *religion* was the answer.

Birsa wanted to unite the Adivasis through a single, positive idea. His knowledge of Christianity and Vaishnavism, stories from the

Bible, and all that he had learnt in school and from various learned people, made him start talking about the concept of a new dawn and freedom from oppression.

He began to preach lessons on life and telling everyone that all was not lost yet.

'There is no need to give up hope. Some day, very soon, we'll be able to establish our own rule again,' said Birsa.

'Is it true? When will the day arrive?' the Mundas asked.

'The day will come, but for that, we all must make sacrifices,' Birsa said.

Sacrifices? What sacrifices?

'We already offer sacrifices to the Sing Bonga,' someone said.

'Animals should not be killed as religious

sacrifices. You have to give up your bad habits, too,' Birsa said.

Give up bad habits, and start a new life, Birsa advised. Only new ideas, new habits, cleansing the body and soul can bring a sea change in your lives, Birsa said. In order to achieve the day when life would be free from struggle and pain, one must stop the sacrifice of animals on religious occasions, stop drinking liquor, stop lying and begging, keep the body and homes clean and love everyone.

It was a brilliant new idea!

It was neither a legal step, nor a political one. Legal petitions and protests had failed to stop the oppression of landlords and reduce their tax burdens. This was social reform—a change in the thinking and in the lives of his people. It was like cleansing themselves in order to take on the evil.

Birsa's words had a huge impact.

Thousands of people from different parts of the region came and gathered at Chalkad. They wanted to believe in this 20-year-old man's words. They wanted to accept him as their leader who could lead them from the front.

His speeches had people engrossed, and as word spread, many from adjoining villages came to see him. People were more and more convinced that Birsa could save them from the clutches of the landlords. He won over people in several surrounding villages like Kuria, Tubil, Muchia, Birbanki and so on.

As people started trusting him and followed his advice, Birsa's image gradually changed into that of a religious preacher, whose words magnetically attracted people. They listened to him awe-struck.

Soon, he came to be known as Dharti Aba or the father of the earth. As his teachings continued, bit by bit, Birsa's own religion—Birsaism—was born. Those who followed him, came to be known as the Birsaites. The messenger of god had become god himself. Some people even approached him as Sing Bonga himself, or the Sun god, a good spirit who kept watch over them.

People felt good listening to his speeches of hope and promise. They were relieved that all was not lost.

His influence over the people increased and some Sardars became involved in his activities

and slowly, a movement of sorts began that had, at its core, religious faith and beliefs. But a deep grudge and sorrow, anger and discontent against the British rulers was also very much alive in the Adivasis.

Sometimes, Birsa Munda is presented in some records as a religious leader before becoming a full-fledged political leader leading a courageous Adivasi army. The Adivasi society of 19th-century India was going through a massive crisis due to the new political system and new laws of agriculture and land. Birsa's prophesies and messages brought huge relief to the impoverished and depressed Mundas. There finally seemed a way out.

Birsa's ideas were new and radical. He questioned age-old customs, beliefs and practices and asked people to get rid of superstition, prohibited begging and told people to worship one god. He aimed to bring different Adivasis under a common set of ideas and principles.

The Sardars could not unite them through politics but Birsa's preaching did that. He brought hope in his message. Much later, it would all change. And from a religious movement it would become a forceful political movement in the form of guerrilla war.

How was the young leader of the masses viewed by those against whom he was building this massive movement?

The missionaries said he was a 'fraud'. The British officers, landlords and missionaries all felt threatened by this new leader. They had never been questioned before. There had hardly been any powerful 'leader' of the Adivasis in the region. And here was a young man, educated in a missionary school, who spoke well and the people loved him. What could be more threatening?

A counter campaign was launched against Birsa. When we look at the records and books on Birsa Munda, some of them project him as a madman. In these records, his valour is ridiculed as madness, his protest is seen as trouble-making.

As Birsa Munda started gaining more and more followers, in August-end 1895, he and some of his followers were arrested by the British police. Would it be the end of Birsa Munda?

Chapter Four

Stories of a new magician-messiah-healer-saviour flew thick and fast and soon reached the police. This was not good, they knew, if people preferred to obey and follow the words of someone else other than them. This excitement and support had to be squashed at the earliest. The deputy commissioner of Ranchi ordered Birsa to appear for a hearing. The complaint was that villagers were neglecting their duties on the fields. But Birsa did not appear before him. He had long announced before his followers that the Sarkar's rule (the British rule) had ended.

The police, on hearing this 'announcement', sent a head constable to Chalkad. He reached there in the first week of August 1895, on a dark and rainy day. He could do nothing. The next morning, he got hold of Birsa. But the Birsaites pounced on the constable and drove him away. As the policemen fled, Birsa's followers laughed and shouted and celebrated.

To the police, this event was both extraordinary and insulting.

Though Birsa had asked his followers to not get too carried away, there were rumours that a massive uprising was about to take place. There were talks and whispers that Birsa was preparing for an armed attack with balaws (axes), lathis (sticks), bows and arrows and had asked people to gather at Chalkad. It was not clear who had spread these rumours.

Even as the final week of August 1895 approached, the British could not arrest Birsa. The British police tried hard to show people that he was a madman. The commissioner wanted him to be put away, proclaimed a lunatic, or as someone who had disturbed the peace. The district superintendent of police, G.R.K. Meares, with a warrant in hand to arrest Birsa and nine of his followers for preventing a public servant (the head constable) from carrying out his duties, left for Bandgaon on an elephant. Twenty armed police personnel followed them on foot. Reverend Lusty of the Anglican Mission was also a part of this team, on the elephant along with

G.R.K. Meares. They travelled on broken roads and difficult terrain and eventually reached Chalkad in the late afternoon.

The officers and foot-soldiers were all tired by then, not being accustomed to travelling in such conditions. But they had a very important job at hand. Some of them walked stealthily and reached right up to Birsa's house. Others kept guard at a distance and gradually surrounded the house. Two policemen entered Birsa's room where he was fast asleep. The police quietly slipped handcuffs on him and that was it! Birsa Munda had been arrested. He was no king, no magician! How else could the police arrest him?

Birsa screamed and tried hard to free himself. But it was impossible. Hearing Birsa's screams, about ten of his followers came rushing. But they were stopped by the police. Reverend Lusty spoke to the people in Mundari and asked them to calm down, and Birsa was taken away.

People were shocked and heartbroken. Here they were preparing for a Munda Raj, but their leader was gone.

From Chalkad, Birsa was taken to Bandgaon. And from there he was rushed to Ranchi and produced before the deputy commissioner. Many of Birsa's followers went to Ranchi where he was put on trial.

It was here that the police saw how much Birsa was loved by the people! During the trial, the court room was overflowing with people. The huge impact Birsa had on the people was clear to the British administration.

They were trying hard to prove Birsa a madman, but he kept his cool and asked his followers to not get swayed by these rumours. A story goes that when Birsa was taken to jail, a thick mud wall collapsed. People started saying that this showed that god was angry. This could have been one of the Sardars' stories to make sure that Birsa's followers did not lose heart.

After weeks of trial, Birsa and some of his followers were convicted on 19 November 1895 for rioting and were sentenced to two years of imprisonment. The verdict made the British police happy. A rowdy and a madman was not going to trouble them anymore. If he somehow managed to survive the tortuous life in jail, he would be too broken to lead a movement again. The judgement read that it deserved 'unusual congratulation that the movement was successfully extinguished'.

How wrong they were!

Little did the government, police, landlords, missionaries and moneylenders apprehend how forceful the movement was going to get from here on. It would sprout and bloom again, because after all, the lives of the Mundas hadn't changed. Neglect and hunger continued to ravage their lives. The days ahead involved the same hard work, sweat and blood. How could a rebellion not form when it had all these ingredients?

Meanwhile, discontent and anger brewed and simmered in Birsa's heart for two long years while he was in jail. Many think that Birsa Munda's arrest perhaps helped strengthen the movement of the Mundas. It increased their conviction, and they could clearly work out the path they ought to take ahead.

Birsa was transferred to the Hazaribagh jail where he was imprisoned for two years.

He was released in 1897, a year that marked the Diamond Jubilee of Queen Victoria, which was celebrated across the country.

The two years in prison gave Birsa enough time to think hard on the way ahead. Would it be a religious movement or an armed war? Once outside the jail, he didn't have to think hard, as the events that unfolded before him showed him the way.

> Birsa and his followers could see that hundreds of Adivasis were dying from famine in the Chhotanagpur belt while many cities in India were celebrating the Diamond Jubilee of Queen Victoria. The famines of 1896-97 and 1899-1900 had brought untold suffering, and the people were waiting to explode. The first famine had affected Khunti, Sisai and Basia areas and the next one affected Sisai and Basia. These areas soon became the main centres of Birsa's movement.

In the years following Birsa's release from jail in 1897, though the movement seemed non-existent on the surface, it was in reality brewing and becoming stronger, waiting to strike forcefully. During the famines, Birsa and some of his close associates worked hard to bring relief to people. He was seen as someone who had gone to jail for the people and worked only for their good. This young man was their only hope. This is how the grains of the ulgulan—an uprising— were sown, though some more time was required for it to take its final shape and explode.

Over the next couple years, the quiet revolution brewed. Meetings were held in the homes of Birsa's followers, or in the depths of forests and hilly areas. Both women and men attended these. Several 'secret places' were identified for the meetings so that no one other than the Birsaites knew of them.

One of the first meetings was held at Bortodih, in the house of his disciples Donka Munda and Sali. Birsa Munda and his core followers came here to chalk out their plans for the future. How would they bring people together? How would they seek their support? What would be the nature of their protest? From where would they gather weapons? How would they strike and from where?

They planned how they would increase the number of Birsaites. There were two distinct paths before them now. One group, led by Soma Munda, wanted to unite people through religion. The other wanted to organize a political revolt. This group was led by Donka Munda.

Which way should they choose?

Initially, it was a combination of both. However, gradually, the focus shifted to an armed movement and an army of warriors was created by the Birsaites.

The Birsaites also visited their sacred places

in order to collect some relics of their ancestral religion and three such relics were brought from three different places. During one such visit to a temple in a place called Chutia, Birsa was spotted by some guards and subsequently an arrest warrant was issued for him. This was the first time since his release from jail that Birsa's activity had caught the attention of the police. But he could not be arrested.

Birsa's followers had spread to various parts of the region. They organized Adivasi people from various parts of the Chhotanagpur belt. Secret war zones were also created in various 'spots' in forests and hilly terrain, which were easy hiding places and also familiar terrain for the Mundas. If the British went there, they would be at a disadvantage.

One such place was the Sail Rakab village in the Dombari Buru (hill) region. It was a hilly and forested terrain filled with rocks and tall trees that could act as hiding places. Strong young men and women had been picked for the Birsaites' army. Organizational responsibilities were divided amongst the most reliable followers such as Donka Munda, Gaya Munda, Dimka Munda, Tatiram Munda and Risha Munda.

The plan was to go for an all-out armed attack on the authorities. The guerrilla army had been formed.

Chapter Five

The movement was now centred around Dombari, rather than Chalkad. Dombari became the place associated with Birsa, the freedom fighter-warrior.

The area is surrounded by hills on all sides and opens into a valley. It was an ideal meeting point, hidden away by the hills. Moreover, it also had a water source close by, a very important consideration when planning an attack. The warriors hiding there for days would need water to drink and for cooking and bathing.

Dombari was also the centre of Hasada country, where the villages are estimated to be about 300 years old. The Mundas see the Hasada area as 'pure'. Here, Munda language and culture dominated, and other influences were much less. On the other hand, the adjoining Naguri area had seen the influence of other cultures and Hindi had got mixed with the local language. These two areas were considered two 'cultural zones' of the Munda territory. The valleys of Icha Hurung, Lango Lor, Domba Ghat and others had been part of Munda folk songs that narrated the imaginary victory of the Mundas against the British.

All these factors together contributed to making Dombari the centre of the Munda uprising against the British in 1897-1900.

Meetings were held in the early months of 1898. At a meeting in Simbua during the festival of Holi, nearly 300 Birsaites gathered with bows and arrows. They lit a huge bonfire and danced. Through their songs and dances, they encouraged each other to overcome fear.

Birsa Munda declared that they should end the kingdom of Ravana (the British) and burn the effigy of Mandodari (the British queen). A plantain tree was set on fire. Birsa called upon his disciples to chop it off and one of his followers cut it down with a huge blow.

Another meeting was held at Dombari hill a week ahead of the Sohrai festival of 1899—the harvest festival in the Bihar, Jharkhand, Odisha and the Bengal region. Here, Birsa raised two flags, one white, that represented the Mundas, and another red, symbolizing the dikus, or outsiders. Birsa took out a sword, announced a war cry, and dealing a blow at the red flag said that the ground would soon turn red with the blood of the dikus.

Birsa went from place to place addressing his followers and prepared them for war. He wore a sacred thread and tied a dhoti, as his clothing. The Mundas recognized him for what he was—a simple villager and a warrior leader. The few photographs of Birsa Munda that one can find, show he had bright eyes, and that his persona was a combination of the many influences on him—a spiritual leader who was also a warrior. People trusted and worshipped him like god. They would do anything he asked for, even lay down their lives for him.

Soon, many more meetings were held all over the region and beyond. Lohardaga, Khunti, Bundu, Tamar, Porahat areas in Singhbhum, among others. Birsa operated from the depths of forest and hilly regions. The Birsaites organized their arms training in deep forests. Both the leaders and foot-soldiers practised warfare skills for hours. They were not just dedicated fighters but loyal Birsaites who were pledged to the cause of bringing about Munda Raj by ending the British rule. Sword fighting, shooting with bows and arrows, running, traversing the difficult terrain were all practised so they could be fit and always fearless.

On 22 December 1899, Birsa held a meeting in Singhbhum with sixty senior members. Here, a grand preparation was planned for an attack on Christmas Eve. Birsa spoke of the oppression they faced and how it had to be avenged. He assigned specific responsibilities to different followers. Dore was deputed to Karaikela, Kali to Chaibasa, Chamon to Chakradharpur, Soma to Bandgaon, Molgu to Sangra and Borai to Kundrugutu.

It had been two years since Birsa was released from prison, the planning was meticulous. It was time to strike and the ulgulan to begin. The great uprising of 1899-1900 was all about asserting that the Mundas were the true owners of the land.

The British police had a good system of collecting information, and had some idea of an attack being planned for Christmas Eve. But they failed to understand the seriousness of the threat. The government had information that Birsa Munda might 'resurface'. For years, he hadn't done any 'mischief', but they thought he would reappear. How would he do so? Would he strike at all? Or was it just baseless fear?

The Deputy Commissioner of Ranchi sent a Mundari-speaking inspector and some constables in disguise to pick up clues from the ground. The District Superintendent of Police went to make enquiries himself. And in December 1899, the Deputy Commissioner himself went on a tour to find out the truth. However, he had to return to Ranchi to attend a conference. All sorts of rumours were flying, but he failed to pick up the clues on the trouble ahead.

On Christmas Eve, as planned, the Birsaites attacked several areas of Singhbhum, Khunti and Ranchi. Village churches and mission houses were targeted, as were people associated with them. The largest number of attacks were in Khunti where houses were burnt. The Murhu Anglican School building where Reverend Lusty was listening to hymns was attacked. He had been behind Birsa's arrest four years earlier. Reverend Lusty, however, was not hurt. The attackers set fire to a building of the Sarwada Mission. Reverend Hoffman and Reverend Carbery, who were inside the bungalow at that time, rushed out on seeing the fire and were attacked. Reverend Carbery was hit on the chest, but the injury was not serious. In other places some police personnel were attacked and died as a result. Other laypeople were also hurt. Almost seven thousand Birsaites, both men and women, armed with traditional weapons, attacked Christianized Mundas, missionaries, churches, shopkeepers and others. Police personnel, landlords and merchants were attacked, too. Houses and churches were burnt. This continued till 7 January 1900.

The British needed to gain control quickly now. They had underestimated the power and planning of the Birsaites. They sent two companies of military to quell the movement. In the first few days, they had not realized how organized and well planned the attacks were. H.C. Streatfield, Deputy Commissioner of Police, Ranchi, along with another officer, Captain Roche, and a troop of police constables headed towards the areas where the action was taking place. The smartly dressed officers instantly inspired confidence in the junior officers. They appeared far superior to the silly bumpkin Birsaites, they thought. 'And the leader of the pack—Birsa Munda—the madman, he will be arrested in no time,' the officers said with supreme confidence.

But when they reached Bandgaon and spoke to the local people, the Deputy Commissioner and his team realized that the Birsaites were quite a strong force. H.C. Streatfield decided that a large area in Singhbhum, Khunti and Tamar had to be guarded. Police guards filled these places. A hundred personnel from the military police were rushed to the area from nearby Dumka and Chinsura. Apart from guarding houses, marching on roads, and waiting to counter the Munda attacks, the police also started a massive search operation. The main person on their lookout: Birsa Munda.

As the searches spread in the forests and villages, the police found that the men were mostly missing. Where had they gone? It was evident that the men of these homes were involved in the attack, and that they had prior information that the police were coming. But there was no trace of Birsa Munda anywhere. He and his associates had vanished. The Birsaites had a good information network, and the strong backing of the ordinary people who had helped them to escape.

Birsa and his followers were, in fact, in the Khunti area, making preparations for another attack. The initial attack had won over many Mundas who had earlier converted to

Christianity. The Birsaites said that they would no longer hurt any Munda but attack only the Sarkar (the government) and urged all villagers to join the cause.

In the village of Etkedih, nearly eighty Birsaites gathered by the river. The police arrived and headed to the riverside. Gaya Munda, of the village, saw the police arriving and alerted the Birsaites by calling out, *'samare hijulenako mar goekope'* (the Sambhar deer have arrived, kill them).

The police party started to cross the river. One of them, Jayram, headed towards the jungle. Gaya Munda's son Sanre shot an arrow at Jayram which struck him and he fell. While some of the police managed to escape, Jayram died almost immediately. This was a huge symbolic victory as a representative of the state had been killed. When the Birsaites, led by Gaya Munda, returned home, the women welcomed them and the men sang hunting songs.

For the police though, it was a shocking news. They realized they were facing an organized guerilla warfare. H.C. Steatfield, the Deputy Commissioner of Ranchi, rushed to the village and on 6 January, reached Gaya Munda's house. He asked the family to surrender but Gaya Munda refused to surrender, and asked H.C. Streatfield to leave his house immediately.

At this, the police set his house on fire. But the family was not frightened, nor did they cower before the police. In fact, the entire family—

including the women—all fought bravely. Gaya Munda's wife Maki, two daughters-in-law, three daughters along with their children put up a brave front. Maki attacked a police sub-inspector. But eventually, a few villagers with their traditional weapons could not overpower the police with their huge force and firepower.

The police had no idea where the next attack was going to happen. The Birsaites had planned an attack in Khunti and it was going to be a show of strength. They brandished swords and bows and arrows and shouted slogans like *'Khunti re rahar jaromakana, dolabu maea'* (the rahar crop in Khunti is ripe, let us harvest it).

They headed towards Khunti police station, as the building represented power and authority. They gave a war cry—the kulkuli—as they closed in on the police station and aimed arrows and pelted it with stones.

Initially, the police in the station were stunned, and many ran away. Then, they retaliated by firing at the attackers. Many policemen ran amok, unable to figure out how to handle the situation. A constable was severely injured and died later. How many Birsaites were injured or killed in this attack is not clear. They also set fire to a building in the police station premises and some houses in the vicinity and set some horses free from the police station.

As the flames licked the walls of the building, it reflected the smouldering rage within the hearts of the Mundas. This rage could turn everything around into ashes. To the British government it was now finally clear that this was no child's play or madman's whims they were dealing with. It was a well-planned attack, nothing short of an armed insurrection.

Chapter Six

Rumours were flying that the town of Ranchi would be attacked next. The landlords, moneylenders and the other rich people were shaken. People were afraid to step out after dark. Would *they* be the next target of the Mundas? The British administration was rattled, too. They had not expected such a coordinated plan from someone they saw as a petty troublemaker.

Four hundred soldiers, police officers, constables and volunteers set about patrolling the roads at all hours. Armed guards stood ready. But Ranchi wasn't attacked.

Deputy Commissioner Streatfield, along with Captain Roche and several police personnel headed to the Saiko area on receiving information that the Birsaites were hiding there and planning another attack from there. Nothing happened that night. The Commissioner of Police, Chhotanagpur, Mr Forbes, reached Saiko the next morning and joined the other officers. Now someone told them that the Birsaites had gathered around Sail Rakab village in the Dombari Buru hill region.

Was it true? And if so, were they armed? They must be, thought Forbes.

'It must be suppressed with such force, that they will never raise their heads again,' Forbes thought. Forbes was bursting with anger and excitement as he led his team to Sail Rakab.

On 9 January 1900, moving stealthily through the thickly forested and hilly terrain, the police team finally could see Dombari Buru at a distance. They waited with bated breath. Was it true that thousands of Mundas had gathered there? Were they hiding there, waiting to attack?

Sure enough, they were there! The Birsaites were hiding behind the rocks and rugged surfaces of Dombari Buru. The police had surrounded them stealthily from all sides. They had crawled through the forested areas, then moved towards the stream without making the slightest noise. The water kept flowing in low murmurs and somewhere at a distance, a bird shrieked. The echo tore through the silence.

Would Sail Rakab turn into a battlefield?

The Birsaites seemed well prepared. This was the day they had been waiting for, when they would assert themselves and restore their pride. Some people believe in non-violence. And yet, armed insurrections have taken place through history. People have resorted to guerilla warfare when all peaceful means have failed. The Mundas took to violence only after generations of their people had been deprived and tortured, and their demands made through peaceful means had been ignored. Then they stood up in protest, carrying arms, with tears in their eyes and fire in their hearts.

Gone was the time when they had filed petitions, pleaded for taxes to be reduced, prayed for their land rights to be restored. All this had brought them only humiliation and a further erosion of their rights. The Birsaites wanted their rights. And they wanted respect. They were going to get these back now—with weapons, bloodshed, and by laying down their lives. For generations after, people would know how they had been pushed into poverty and how they had refused to be humiliated any longer. This ulgulan was going to be remembered forever and by all.

> Birsaites composed and sang many songs. One of the songs narrates how outsiders took away the Mundas' khuntkatti rights and that Birsa Bhagwan had come to help them reclaim it. In the song they express their willingness to sacrifice their lives and inspires others to assemble with bows and arrows to fight the battle to get back their 'happy land':
>
> *...Today for us death is better than life.*
> *Birsa Bhagwan is our leader*
> *He has come down for us in the land*
> *Today...*

Let us get ready with the quiver, arrow and sword,
We shall assemble on the Dombari hill,
The Father of the Earth speaks up there.
We shall not be afraid of the monkeys
We shall not spare the zamindars, moneylenders
   and shopkeepers
They occupied our land.
We shall not give up our khuntkatti rights.
From (the jaws of) leopards and snakes, we
   reclaimed our land.
The happy land was seized by the enemies.

Hundreds of rebels had assembled at Sail Rakab. When the police force was quite near, the Birsaites started waving their arms while still hiding. An officer called out to them, and an interpreter translated his words to Mundari, asking them to lay down their arms and surrender. The police wanted Birsa Munda to surrender. 'End your revolt here, right now,' the interpreter called out.

But the Mundas had not announced a guerilla war just to surrender. This battle would be fought till the very end. They challenged the police in turn. If anyone was to lay down arms and surrender, it should be the police, they said. They continued to brandish their arms and refused to hand over their leader Birsa.

One of the Birsaites, Narsingh Munda, shouted to the officers that the right to rule over their kingdom was the Mundas' alone. So it was the British who should lay down their arms, surrender and give in. 'If you do not lay down your arms, if you don't give up the Raj, be prepared to fight till the end,' Narsingh Munda told the British.

The British officers were shocked. They were not prepared for such audacity! Forbes now commanded his men to prepare to strike. The officers strategized on the best possible way to get the Birsaites. After weighing various possibilities, the police decided to open fire from a distance. The Birsaites were unperturbed. The initial volley of fire let loose by a large number of British soldiers firing simultaneously in the direction of the Mundas, had no impact. It didn't hit anyone. The Mundas responded with cries to show they were invincible. Some hid behind the rocks, while others began to hurl stones, or aimed arrows at the police. Now, a second barrage of firing was aimed at the Birsaites. This time, a few Munda warriors fell.

The Mundas quickly recovered and kept throwing stones at the police. A third volley was fired at them. Some more Mundas fell this time but most continued to throw stones and shouted, challenging the British soldiers. They were full of power and courage as they flaunted their axes, swords, bows and arrows that gleamed in the sunlight.

By now, the police had begun to climb up and were circling closer. Their firing continued unabated. A volley of stones came their way but a few stones could not stop the police. With their guns they could strike at the Birsaites from a distance and remain unhurt. As they got closer and closer to the hiding spots of the Munda army, they shot three women. More firing, more Mundas dropped dead. Some of them came running towards the British soldiers with arrows and spears. But they were no match to the firepower of the British policemen. Blood seeped into the soil, then it trickled down the hill. Bodies of the Mundas lay all over Sail Rakab, and the ground was wet with the blood of the brave warriors.

The Munda warriors had been defeated. But the police continued their killing, and women and children lay dead as well. Later, the officers claimed that they didn't know about the presence of women as they wore the same kind of clothes as the men and both men and women sported long hair. Some records say that twenty Birsaites were killed. Some say many more died.

But where was Birsa Munda?

The search began. The British police combed the forests, hills and village after village to locate the leader of the masses, their Dharti Aba, their Bhagwan. They found a large number of weapons as well as cooking vessels, rice and other food, indicating that the Birsaite warriors had well planned their attack and were prepared for a long haul. But there was no sign of Birsa. Unless the supreme leader was found, the operation by the British soldiers could hardly be called a 'success'. So he had to be nabbed.

According to some, Birsa had escaped into

the depths of the forest after putting up a brave fight at Sail Rakab. His followers had helped him escape, for if Birsa was caught, their war would come to an end immediately. If Birsa could hide for some time and evade the police, then they would organize themselves again and the fight would continue till they established the Munda Raj.

Birsa first hid at Bortodih, where some followers guarded him. Birsa was restless. The cries of his warriors kept echoing in his mind, the visions of blood at Sail Rakab kept coming back, tormenting him.

How many of his people had died! How much they suffered! What would he do staying alive, thought Birsa. 'The Mundas must strike again,' he thought, sitting on a charpoy in the middle of the forest. His followers were guarding him from all sides.

He thought of bringing together hundreds of Birsaites again and they would attack the sahibs. Flames would lick their walls, blood would flow from their institutions, and the Munda Raj would be established.

Amid the bloodshed, death and silence, Birsa had a sudden realization which filled him with a calm. Hadn't the warfare been a success, after all? How the police officers ran from one part of the forest to another! How they were caught off guard! Their buildings were in flames. They had understood the reasons for the attack. They were afraid that the Mundas may strike again. Hundreds of soldiers were guarding their homes and combing the forests relentlessly. Birsa's warfare tactics were a success!

The uprising was spread over a thousand square kilometres of the hilly region, and several incidents took place over 95 kilometres apart. It was no mean achievement. The impact of this uprising would be felt far and wide. People would remember them forever. He would organize the Mundas again and the fight would continue. Even if he were caught soon, they would strike again.

The hide-and-seek continued for some more time. The hills and forests hid Birsa for a long time, protecting him. But bit by bit, the British started getting closer to him. From Bortodih, Birsa headed towards Ayubhatu, his mother's village. There, he stayed for a few days. But it soon became difficult to trust anyone. The British officers had announced a reward for anyone who gave information on his whereabouts.

'How can I blame the Mundas? The sahibs have shown their true colours by giving the poor bait of money to capture me,' thought Birsa.

It was true. Unable to locate Birsa, the British police announced a reward of five hundred rupees to find Birsa. Any Munda who helped the British in arresting Birsa would also be given rent-free land in their village. These baits worked and that's how the police were able to get on the right trail. When the police reached Ayubhatu, Birsa had already escaped—in disguise—to Maranghada and from there, to Singhbhum.

By now, the police officers had become

restless. Would Birsa and his men strike again? Or would they succeed in capturing him? The commissioner himself went to Bandgaon to conduct the operations. The Deputy Commissioner of Singhbhum headed towards some Birsaite villages like Kareka, Tukadih, Chatuma, Sinko, Kodadiha, Katamkel and so on. The police picked up about forty-seven Birsaites. Some were arrested, while others—thirty-five of them—were released. This made people afraid.

During these search operations, the tribals fought bravely to resist the police. But the British started using more and more harsh ways to extract information.

They decided to evict some Birsaites from their land and replaced them with those who had helped the government. They cut off food supplies to the Birsaites' villages. Slowly, many important Birsaites were arrested. As Birsa continued to evade the police, his people faced more and more brutality and the atmosphere was filled with fear and hopelessness.

Though none of his closest allies gave away information on Birsa's whereabouts, it was difficult for him to keep hiding and moving from one place to another as the villagers could no longer be trusted as before. They were afraid and under pressure from the British.

Chapter Seven

The British government's plan to use Mundas against Mundas definitely worked, even if not immediately. Some Mundas gave in to the pressure.

All this while, Birsa moved from one place to another. He couldn't go very far in any case. The question of moving to any of the big towns or cities away from Chhotanagpur did not arise. He had to hide amid the forests and in the homes of his own people. But how long could he trust them and for how long could he hide?

Some local men of the villages Manmaru and Jarikel began to comb the forests in search of Birsa. They saw smoke coming from the depths of the forests. Slowly crawling on the ground towards it, they got closer and found something moving. Were those humans or some wild animals? Those were certainly humans and the fire was a sure giveaway. They found a group of huts, and in one of them was none other than Birsa Munda himself! There were two women around, lighting fire, cooking and washing.

They could not believe their luck! Only, Birsa had two swords by his side, and the two women were on guard. Their eyes darted this way and that. They looked strong and brave, and clearly they were guarding their Dharti Aba with utmost dedication.

The villagers waited and waited till Birsa had eaten his meal and gone off to sleep. After some time, the women were no longer visible. By now, they were sure that Birsa would be fast asleep. They crept closer to the hut where Birsa was sleeping. Yes, he was there, fast asleep. They pounced on him and overpowered him immediately, before he could fight back.

Birsa was taken to the Deputy Commissioner of Singhbhum. The British were no doubt elated, but now they had to make sure that Birsa was removed as far as possible from his people. He had to be taken somewhere the Birsaites could not reach him. The Deputy Commissioner was asked to send Birsa to Ranchi.

The news of Birsa's arrest spread like wildfire. His followers wept. They had wanted to guard their Dharti Aba with their lives, and soon, they had hoped, they would rise again with Birsa's guidance.

They came out in large numbers at Bandgaon. Birsa's sister Champa and brother-in-law Rasai were there too. As Birsa was being taken away, scores of people stood along the road to take a look at the brave warrior leader. Birsa smiled his beatific smile, wearing a big turban and a sheet covering his body. He was calm as ever.

This gave the Mundas a flicker of hope. Birsa was only twenty-five years old. He could lead them again after he was out of prison. Hadn't it happened earlier too? They went back home, filled with hope amid the despair. Birsa Bhagwan, their god, would make their lives better for sure.

They weren't entirely wrong, though it didn't happen in the way they had visualized it.

> Another song of the Birsaites, mentioning the arrest of their Dharti Aba, that brings out their ache and suffering as he was being taken away, goes like this:
>
> *Oh Birsa, they arrested you...*
> *Oh Birsa, they took you by Ranchi Road...*
> *Oh Birsa, for the land you suffered...*
> *Oh Birsa, you will come back again in the next life...*
> *Oh Birsa, I grieve that they arrested you,*
> *I grieve that they took you away*

Birsa Munda was lodged in a solitary cell in prison. According to some records, on 20 May, food was taken for him at around 5.20 a.m. He was then taken to the court prison along with nineteen other prisoners close to 6 a.m. In the court, he fell very ill all of a sudden and was taken back to the jail. Some medicines were given to him close to 10 in the morning.

He was very sick for three days, and doctors said that he was suffering from cholera and may not survive. The Deputy Commissioner asked the jail superintendent, Captain A.R.S. Anderson, to see if he could do anything. Birsa's health apparently improved till 7 June, but then it deteriorated on 8 June. On 9 June 1900, he died.

Many say that the death was suspicious and he was either tortured and killed or poisoned in prison, and Jail Superintendent Anderson was behind this. It is said that he even asked the jailor to write that Birsa had died from cholera.

This official cause of death as issued by Captain Anderson was challenged by the Evangelical Mission of Chhotanagpur, who suggested poisoning either by the police authorities or by the sardars. Whatever the truth, none can deny that for the British colonial rulers, Birsa Munda staying alive meant that the movement would remain thriving. After all, to the entire Munda community, Birsa was a living god and a fighter who was fighting for their cause.

Whatever may have happened within the confines of the prison, it is important to remember that the idea of Birsa Munda continued to live on even after his death.

Many Birsaites were put on trial apart from Birsa Munda himself. Out of 482 accused in Ranchi and Singhbhum, ninety-eight were convicted, sixty-eight were 'bound down' to keep peace and 296 were acquitted, discharged or pardoned.

The death sentence was given to Gaya Munda and his son Sanre. Others were sentenced to 'transportation for life' (the convicted prisoner was sent off to a prison somewhere else), or given five years' rigorous imprisonment.

But the story of the brave Munda warriors and that of Birsa Munda, their leader, started spreading beyond the Chhotanagpur region. The trial of over 300 Birsaites became national news. Surendra Nath Banerjee, the editor of *The Bengalee* newspaper, criticized the British over 'legal cover-ups and delays'. *The Statesman* alleged that the Birsaites were denied legal aid. Many Calcutta-based nationalists who earlier had paid little or no attention to the plight of the Adivasis, now started speaking up for them and the British institutions that crushed them. This pressure from a powerful section of nationalists had a huge impact, and it led to the Chhotanagpur Tenancy Act of 1908.

This Act assured the Adivasis their land rights. Anyone acquiring land in the khuntkattidar village forcibly could be evicted legally. Several villages were restored as

Mundari khuntkatti villages. In villages where a zamindar ruled, the land was surveyed and recorded to prevent any further encroachment, and to give the tenant permanent rights over it. Rents were fixed and could not be altered by zamindars without the consent of the revenue officer. The most important part of the Act was restricting outsiders from any ownership of traditionally owned khuntkatti land without permission of the entire village and the district commissioner.

The Mundas got official recognition of their demands, and people believe that the right to land was established as a result of Birsa's rebellion.

Birsa Munda may have died, but that did

A monument at Dombari Buru now commemorates the uprising

not mean the end of what he stood for. Birsa's ideas continue to be practised by many till this day. It has inspired several Adivasi movements and led to the fight against colonial rule in the region. Following Birsa Munda, many indigenous groups started their movements to fight for their rights—the Haribaba Movement of 1930-31 was one such in Singhbhum and Ranchi districts.

Though Birsa's war against the British did not come from a spirit of nationalism, it was about the oppressed fighting against oppressors. And that *is* the spirit of the Indian freedom movement as well! Birsa's war against the British is thus seen as one of the first such protests by Indians.

Birsa is remembered to this day as a social reformer. He is a hero, an icon, and represents Adivasi pride. His fight, to claim one's rights, and to awaken self-respect is remembered well into the 21st century.

Birsa Munda
A Timeline

- 15 November 1875: Birsa Munda is born in Ulihatu (present-day Jharkhand) to Sugana and Karmi Munda. *[There are differences on the date and place of his birth.]*
- 1886 to 1890: Birsa lives in Chaibasa and gets his upper primary education here.
- 1890: Birsa leaves for Bandgaon where he works and comes under the influence of Vaishnavism.

- 1894-95: Birsa turns into a healer, preacher, leader and influences many people.
- August 1895: Birsa Munda is arrested from Chalkad.
- 19 November 1895: Birsa Munda is convicted for rioting and sentenced to two years of imprisonment.
- 1896-97 and 1899-1900: two famines take place in the Chhotanagpur region.
- November 1897: Birsa is released from jail and taken to Chalkad.
- February-March 1898: Meetings are organized by Birsa Munda in the homes of his followers to chalk out the path ahead.
- 22 December 1899: Birsa holds a meeting in Singhbhum with sixty senior members.

- 24 December 1899 to 7 January 1900: Birsa leads the attack on the British, Christian missionaries, landlords and those siding with them, the dikus or outsiders in Singhbhum, Khunti areas.
- 9 January 1900: Birsaites and British soldiers fight a pitched battle at Sail Rakab in Dombari Buru. Birsa is helped by his followers to escape from there.
- 3 February 1900: Birsa is arrested.
- 20 May 1900: Birsa falls sick in prison. He is said to be suffering from cholera.
- 9 June 1900: Birsa Munda dies.

Author's Note

Birsa Munda took a firm stand against the British at a time when Adivasis were exploited beyond belief. He dared, he led and he left a mark, showing how the impoverished can lead a movement against the powerful when all peaceful methods of demanding one's rights fail.

I have relied primarily on the book, *Birsa Munda*, by K.S. Singh (published by National Book Trust), for the information on Birsa Munda. It is a fascinating and detailed narrative of the life of Birsa Munda. The two songs mentioned are also from Singh's book. Articles and papers that helped me understand Birsa Munda are *Munda Religion and Social Structure* by Hilary Standing (School of Oriental and African Studies), *Remembering Birsa Munda, the Social Reformer and Revolutionary Leader* by Prabal Saran Agarwal and Harsh Vardhan Tripathy (published in thewire.in) and *Capturing Birsa Munda: The Virtuality of a Colonial-era Photograph*, by Daniel J. Rycroft.

I would like to thank Sudeshna Shome Ghosh and Radhika Shenoy of Talking Cub for their editing of the book. Many thanks to Devashish Verma for the illustrations.

Swati Sengupta

Read more in The Incredible Life series from Talking Cub

The Incredible Life of Milkha Singh
The Runner Who Could Fly

Swati Sengupta

The Incredible Life of
Jhalkari Bai
The Braveheart Warrior

Swati Sengupta

The Incredible Life of Savitribai Phule
The Fearless Reformer

Swati Sengupta